Questions AND Answers

ANCIENT CIVILIZATIONS

Wendy Madgwick

KINGFISHER
Kingfisher Publications Plc
New Penderel House
283-288 High Holborn
London WC1V 7HZ
www.kingfisherpub.com

First published by Kingfisher Publications Plc in 2000
10 9 8 7 6 5 4 3

3TR/0501/TIM/HBM/130MA

A CIP catalogue for this book is available from the British Library

ISBN 0 7534 0480 X

Printed in China

Author: Wendy Madgwick
Designed, edited and typeset: Tucker Slingsby Ltd

Illustrations:
Julian Baker, Sue Barclay, Simone Boni, Peter Bull, Vanessa Card, Stephen
Conlin, Peter Dennis, Francesca D'Ottavi, Angelika Elsebach, Terry Gabbey,
Luigi Galante, Jeremy Gower, Peter Gregory, Ray Grinaway, Alan Hardcastle,
Donald Harley, Nick Harris, Nicholas Hewitson, Adam Hook, Christian Hook,
Ian Jackson, Ruth Lindsay, Kevin Maddison, Janos Marffy, John Marshall, David
McAllister, Angus McBride, Nicki Palin, Mark Pepe, Melvyn Pickering, Bernard
Robinson, Mike Saunders, Mark Stacey, George Thompson,
Wendy Webb, Andrea Wheatcroft, Sohraya Willis, David Wright

Contents

The First Peoples   4

River Valley Civilizations   6

Ancient Egypt   8

Priests and Mummies   10

Pyramids and Tombs   12

Crete and Mycenae   14

Babylon   16

Assyrians and Hittites   18

Ancient Sea Traders   20

Ancient Greece   22

Greek Life   24

The Persians   26

Ancient China   28

The Celts   30

Life in Ancient Rome   32

The Roman Empire   34

The Mayan Empire   36

Timeline   38

Index and Answers   40

The First Peoples

Early humans lived in caves and tents, moving from place to place in search of food. Around 8000 BC people began to grow crops and keep animals. These early farmers settled down and lived in small villages, which later grew larger and became towns and cities.

Who painted caves?

Over 100 cave paintings have been discovered in Europe, some dating back to about 25,000 BC. Rock paintings have been found in Africa and Australia. They were painted by prehistoric people, who used natural pigments to draw animals and hunting scenes.

Which was the largest ancient city?

The largest known ancient city is Çatal Hüyük in present-day Turkey. By 6250 BC, over 6,000 people lived there. The mud-brick houses were one storey high, but they did not have front doors. People entered by climbing a ladder and crawling through a hole in the roof.

What sort of gods did ancient people worship?

The early city-dwellers built religious shrines, but little is known about their gods. This clay figure, found at a decorated shrine in Çatal Hüyük, may have been a mother goddess.

What did the first people hunt?

Stone Age people hunted wild animals for food. One of the largest animals they hunted was the mammoth, a kind of prehistoric elephant. No part of a mammoth was wasted. The flesh fed a group of prehistoric people for weeks. Its furry skin was used to make clothes and tents, and the tusks and bones were used to build huts and carved to make jewellery.

Quick-fire Quiz

1. What was Çatal Hüyük?
a) A country
b) A kind of house
c) A city

2. What was a mammoth?
a) A prehistoric elephant
b) A prehistoric tiger
c) A prehistoric person

3. When were wolves tamed?
a) 2000 BC
b) 10,000 BC
c) 40,000 BC

4. What was made from palm leaves?
a) Rope
b) Paper
c) Bread

What did they eat?

People in Çatal Hüyük ate meat, fruits such as apples, and nuts and vegetables. They also made great use of date palms. They ate the fruit, the tree trunks provided timber, and the leaves were used to roof their houses or were plaited and woven into rope, mats and sandals.

Did the first people keep animals?

People tamed wolves as long ago as 10,000 BC. These were the first domesticated dogs and were used to herd other animals. In time, wild sheep, goats, cows and pigs were kept as farm animals.

Early farm animals

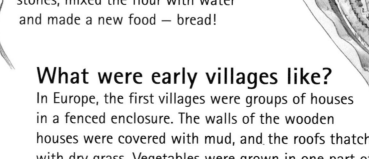

What crops did they grow?

Early farmers sowed wild wheat and barley seeds. A new form of wheat with plumper seeds developed when wild wheat was cross-bred with a kind of grass. The farmers ground these seeds between stones, mixed the flour with water and made a new food — bread!

What were early villages like?

In Europe, the first villages were groups of houses in a fenced enclosure. The walls of the wooden houses were covered with mud, and the roofs thatched with dry grass. Vegetables were grown in one part of the enclosure, and farm animals were kept in another.

River Valley Civilizations

The first great civilization, Sumer, developed in about 5000 BC between the Tigris and Euphrates rivers. The area was later called Mesopotamia (now Iraq). Sumer lasted 3,000 years. In that time, other civilizations grew up along the River Nile in Egypt and the River Indus in Pakistan.

Did the Indus people build cities?

In the 1920s, two cities – Mohenjo-daro and Harappa – were found in the Indus valley. They dated from about 2000 BC, and were built in a grid pattern like modern American cities.

Who invented the wheel?

No-one knows when the wheel was invented. The potter's wheel was used in Mesopotamia about 6,000 years ago. By about 3200 BC the Sumerians were using simple carts like this. Later they had wheeled war chariots which were pulled by donkeys or wild asses.

Who invented writing?

Writing was probably invented by the Sumerians about 5,000 years ago. At first they drew pictures, but later these were turned into wedge-shaped symbols, which we now call cuneiform writing.

What crops did they grow?

Farmers in the Indus valley grew many crops, including wheat, barley, melons, dates and cotton. Each city had a huge, well-aired granary to store the grain between harvests.

Granary in Mohenjo-daro

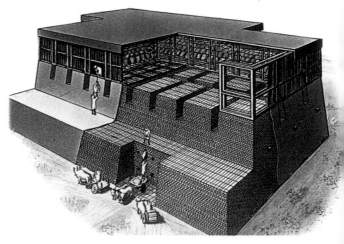

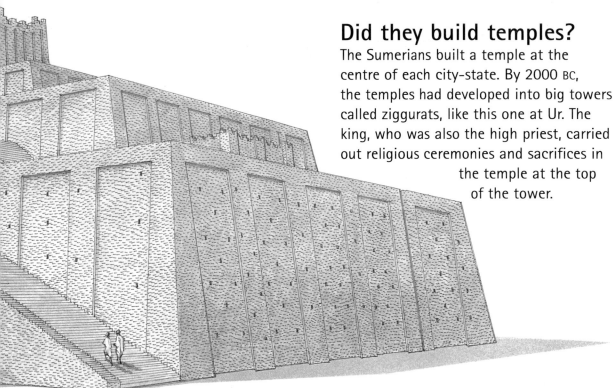

Did they build temples?

The Sumerians built a temple at the centre of each city-state. By 2000 BC, the temples had developed into big towers called ziggurats, like this one at Ur. The king, who was also the high priest, carried out religious ceremonies and sacrifices in the temple at the top of the tower.

Quick-fire Quiz

1. What was a ziggurat?
a) A house
b) A tower
c) A palace

2. What kind of writing did the Sumerians use?
a) Cuneiform
b) Hieroglyphs
c) Letters

3. Where was Harappa?
a) Sumer
b) Egypt
c) Indus valley

4. What did early Sumerians use to build their houses?
a) Wood
b) Stone
c) Reeds

What were river valley homes made from?

Most ancient peoples built homes from the materials around them. The Sumerians had no stones or trees, so they built houses from reeds and, later, sun-dried mud bricks. The Indus people lived in mud-brick houses built around courtyards. Each house had several rooms, a toilet and a well. The Indus civilization lasted 800 years. It came to an end in about 1800 BC.

Did they play games?

Rich Sumerians did not have to work all the time, so they relaxed by listening to music or playing games. This game board, found in a royal grave at Ur, dates from between 3000 and 2000 BC. No-one knows how it was played.

Did the Sumerians have money?

The Sumerians traded at huge markets. Each trader had his own cylinder seal for signing contracts. Sales were recorded on clay tablets. By about 3300 BC, Sumerians were using clay tokens to buy goods. They may have had different sorts of tokens for different kinds of goods.

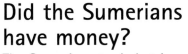

Who ruled Sumer?

Each Sumerian city-state had its own king. A king sometimes took over other cities, but none ever ruled all of Sumer. The royal families were very rich and wore fine clothes. A Sumerian princess wore a long dress with gold and silver jewellery.

Ancient Egypt

Over 5,000 years ago, two Egyptian kingdoms – Upper and Lower Egypt – grew up by the River Nile in North Africa. In 3100 BC, King Menes united Egypt. It became a very powerful empire which lasted until 30 BC, when Egypt fell to the Romans.

Did Egyptians play games?

Like most ancient peoples, wealthy Egyptians spent their leisure time listening to music or playing board games. Their children played with toys including balls, spinning tops, dolls and model animals.

Scribe

Who wrote letters?

Not all Egyptians could read and write. Men called scribes wrote letters for them. Scribes used hieroglyphs (picture writing) for royal and sacred writing, and simplified symbols for business letters. They used reed pens and a kind of paper called papyrus.

How do we know about ancient Egypt?

The remains of tombs, written records and wall paintings have helped build up a picture of ancient Egypt. Wall paintings show religious rituals, royal conquests and scenes of everyday life.

Did they wear wigs?

Yes, the ancient Egyptians thought that hair was dirty, so they shaved their heads and wore fancy wigs. They also wore make-up. They mixed powdered minerals such as lead, copper and iron oxide with water or oils to make bright lipstick, eye shadow and blusher.

How did Egyptians make bread?

Bread was the main food for poor Egyptians. Wheat and barley were ground into flour. They mixed this with water to make a dough, added flavouring such as garlic or honey, and baked it in clay pots.

Were pharaohs rich?

Egyptian kings, called pharaohs, were worshipped and treated like gods. They owned the whole country, and everybody and everything belonged to them, so they were very rich and powerful! The royal family lived in luxury, waited on by hundreds of servants.

Quick-fire Quiz

1. Who united Egypt?
a) King Nile
b) King Menes
c) King Egypt

2. When did Egypt fall to the Romans?
a) 300 BC
b) 30 BC
c) 3 BC

3. What did a scribe do?
a) Make wigs
b) Build tombs
c) Write letters

4. What crop was swapped for goods?
a) Peas
b) Grain
c) Garlic

Was grain used like money?

Grain was one of the most important crops in ancient Egypt. It was used to pay taxes, and was exchanged for other goods. For this reason, the Egyptians developed an accurate balance to weigh grain and other costly goods.

Why was the River Nile important?

The Egyptian empire grew up along the River Nile because it was good farming land. Hardly any rain fell in Egypt, but every July the River Nile flooded, covering the surrounding ground with water and rich black mud. This mud was great for growing crops. The ancient Egyptians learned how to store enough of the flood water in canals to irrigate (water) the fields in the dry season. This meant they produced enough crops to feed their own people and to sell some to other traders. Almost all Egypt's wealth came from farming.

Priests and Mummies

The ancient Egyptians worshipped many gods and believed in life after death. To make sure their spirits could enjoy the afterlife, the Egyptians embalmed (preserved) the bodies of the dead. The priests were very powerful, helping people with sacred works.

Why were tombs robbed?

Robbers plundered tombs for the treasures they contained. Rich Egyptians were buried

with everything they would need in the afterlife – food, clothes, jewellery and even models of servants. Lucky amulets like these were often placed among a mummy's bandages to ward off evil spirits.

Who was mummified?

Making a mummy was expensive. Only the royal family, top officials and priests were mummified. The poor were buried in reed coffins or in holes in the sand. Animals that represented gods and goddesses, such as cats, dogs, crocodiles and baboons, were sometimes mummified. Cats, for example, represented the goddess Bastet.

What is a mummy?

A mummy is a body that has been preserved. The people who made mummies were called embalmers. After being dried out and rubbed with oils, the body was wrapped in bandages as much as five kilometres long! A priest watched over the embalmers as they worked.

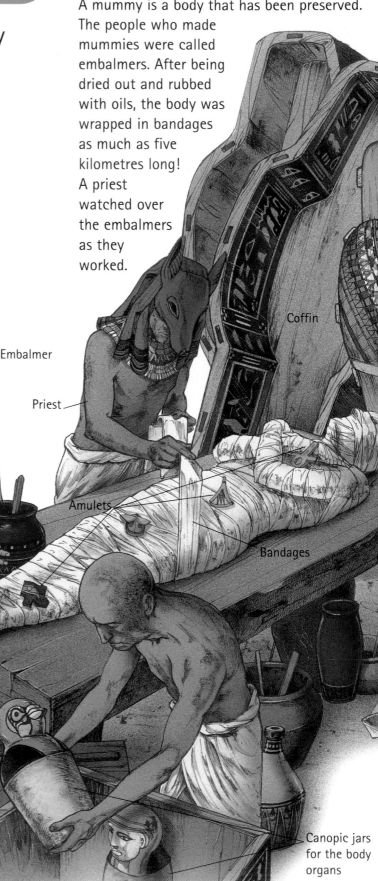

Embalmer

Priest

Coffin

Amulets

Bandages

Canopic jars for the body organs

Which pharaoh's tomb survived?

Most pharaohs' tombs were robbed, but in 1922, archaeologists found the tomb of the young Tutankhamun, who was only 18 when he died. His tomb was still intact and full of priceless treasures, including his mummy and this fabulous golden face mask.

Coffin-painter

What was painted on the coffin?

A body was placed in a nest of two or three coffins, each painted with hieroglyphs (word pictures), gods, pictures of the person's life, and spells to keep away evil spirits.

How was the brain removed?

An embalmer removed the brain by pulling it out through the nostrils with a hooked knife. They did not think the brain was important so they threw it away!

How was a body preserved?

The soft body organs were removed, dried, and placed in vessels called canopic jars. The spaces were packed with rags or sawdust, and the body was stitched up. It was then covered in a kind of salt called natron, which dried it out.

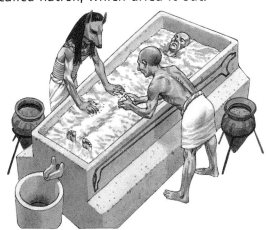

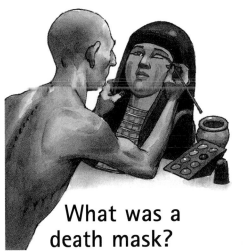

What was a death mask?

A death mask was a portrait of the dead person. It was put over the mummy's face, so that the soul would recognize its body. Death masks were often made of painted wood, but most pharaohs had death masks of beaten gold.

Who wore a jackal's head?

When the priest said the final prayers over a body, he wore a mask to look like the jackal god, Anubis, god of the dead. At the tomb, the priest held the mummy during the 'Opening of the mouth' ceremony, to give the dead person the power to eat, move and breathe.

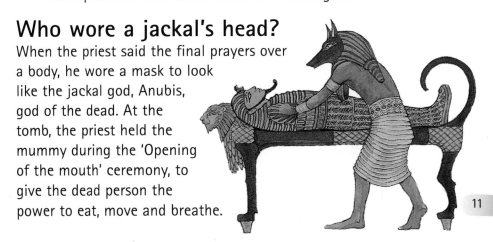

Pyramids and Tombs

Egyptian pharaohs of the Old and Middle Kingdoms (3,500 to 5,000 years ago), were buried under pyramids. In the New Kingdom (3,000 to 3,500 years ago), pharaohs were buried in tombs in a valley on the west bank of the Nile at Thebes.

How was a pyramid built?

It took at least 4,000 craftsmen and thousands of labourers to build a pyramid. The labourers were mostly farmers who worked as builders to pay their taxes. They cleared the site, laid the foundations and dragged the stones into place. Stone masons used an assortment of tools to cut the hard blocks of limestone used to cover the outside of the pyramids. They cut the stone into blocks that fitted together perfectly.

Plumb line

Chisels and hammers

Stone masons

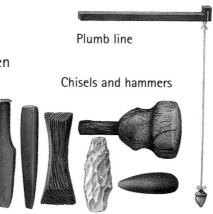

Which temple was moved?

In 1964, the temple at Abu Simbel was moved so that it would not be flooded when the Aswan dam was built. The temple had been carved out of solid rocks on the banks of the River Nile.

Why did Egyptians have funeral barges?

The mummified bodies of Egyptian pharaohs were placed on highly decorated boats so that they could travel to the next world. The boat was dragged to the tomb on a sledge pulled by oxen.

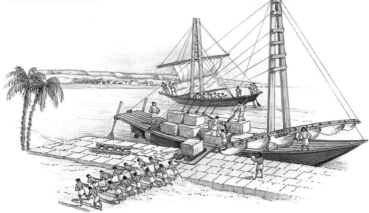

Quick-fire Quiz

1. Where was the Great Pyramid?
a) Thebes
b) Giza
c) Abu Simbel

2. During which Kingdom were the pyramids built?
a) The Old Kingdom
b) All the time
c) The New Kingdom

3. What was built on the west bank of the Nile?
a) Egyptian homes
b) Pharaohs' palaces
c) The pyramids

4. When was the last pyramid built?
a) About 2575 BC
b) About 1570 BC
c) About 570 BC

Where did the stones come from?

The inside of a pyramid was built from soft stone found locally. The outside was covered with smooth limestone from quarries up to 800 kilometres away. Huge blocks of stone, up to 50 tonnes in weight, were loaded onto barges in the flood season and shipped to the building site.

Where were the pyramids built?

The pyramids were all built on the west bank of the Nile. The Egyptians believed this was the land of the dead because it was where the Sun set. They built their homes on the east bank, the land of the living, where the Sun rose.

What is the Great Pyramid?

The Great Pyramid at Giza was built for King Khufu (c. 2575 BC) from over two million stone blocks. The pharaoh was buried in a central chamber.

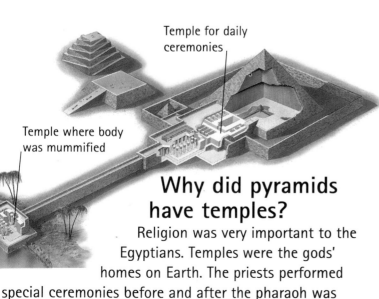

Temple for daily ceremonies

Temple where body was mummified

Why did pyramids have temples?

Religion was very important to the Egyptians. Temples were the gods' homes on Earth. The priests performed special ceremonies before and after the pharaoh was put in the tomb, so temples were built in the pyramids.

Why did pyramid-building stop?

About 90 pyramids were built – the last one in 1570 BC. But they were easy for robbers to get into, so pharaohs of the New Kingdom were buried in tombs carved in the cliffs in a hidden valley at Thebes instead. This is known as the Valley of the Kings. Although most of these tombs were also robbed, it was here that archaeologists Howard Carter and Lord Carnarvon, found the untouched tomb of the boy-king, Tutankhamun.

Crete and Mycenae

The first European civilization began about 4,500 years ago, on the island of Crete. The Minoans, named after a famous king, Minos, were traders who ruled the Aegean Sea. In 1450 BC, this civilization ended and the Mycenaeans, from mainland Greece, took over.

What was the minotaur?

The Minoans told how King Minos kept a minotaur, a monster that was half-man and half-bull, in a labyrinth (maze of tunnels) below his palace. Each year, he sacrificed 14 young Greeks to this terrible creature. The Greek hero, Theseus, was determined to kill the minotaur. With the help of King Minos's daughter, Ariadne, he found a way into the labyrinth, killed the monster and escaped from the maze by following a thread he had unwound on his way through it.

What goods did the Minoans trade?

Craftsmen made beautiful pottery and carved ornaments. Goldsmiths made fine jewellery, such as this bull's head pendant. Minoan goods have been found in many surrounding countries including Egypt.

Did Minoans build cities?

The Minoans built several cities, connected to each other by paved roads. Each had a fine palace. The grandest was at Knossos, in the north of Crete. It had over 1,000 rooms, including luxurious apartments, workshops and a school.

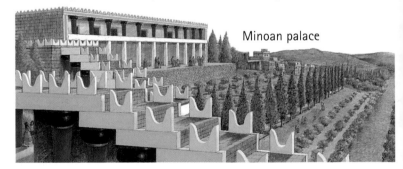

Minoan palace

Who went hunting?

The Mycenaeans loved to hunt wild animals, including lions, which roamed Greece until about 3,000 years ago. This fresco shows a boar hunt. Nobles hunted boar with spears and shields, and had dogs to help them. Hunters cut off the tusks from dead boars, and used them to decorate their helmets.

Did Minoans play sports?

Frescoes (wall-paintings) show the Minoans were very sporty. Boys and girls enjoyed boxing and the dangerous sport of bull-leaping. One person held the bull's head, while the bull-leaper somersaulted between the horns of the bull. A friend stood at the back to catch the acrobat.

What were Mycenaean palaces like?

The Mycenaeans were the ruling Greeks from about 1450 BC until 1100 BC. The remains of the palace of the Mycenaean king Nestor at Pylos, in southern Greece, show that it had richly decorated rooms built around a series of courtyards.

Mycenaean palace

Were the Mycenaeans warriors?

The Mycenaeans, unlike the Minoans, were warriors as well as traders, and built fortified towns. The walls around their city of Mycenae were built from huge stone blocks. At the only entrance, the Lion Gate, a pair of stone lionesses stood guard. Warriors attacked their enemies from the walls.

The Lion Gate

Quick-fire Quiz

1. Which of these civilizations began in Crete?
a) Egyptian
b) Mycenaean
c) Minoan

2. What was the minotaur?
a) Half-man, half-lion
b) Half man, half-bull
c) Half-man, half-boar

3. Who killed the minotaur?
a) King Minos
b) King Nestor
c) Theseus

4. What was the main gate in Mycenae called?
a) The Lion Gate
b) The Bull Gate
c) The King Gate

Babylon

The Mesopotamian city-state of Babylon rose to power in 1900 BC. Hammurabi the Great increased its power in the 1700s BC. It collapsed in 1595 BC, but grew great again under Nebuchadnezzar, 1,000 years later. In 539 BC, Babylon fell to the Persians.

Who made Babylon rich?

Nebuchadnezzar made Babylon one of the richest cities in the world. The main entrance, the Ishtar gate, was covered with glazed blue tiles. He brought plants and trees from Persia for the famous Hanging Gardens, which were one of the 'Seven Wonders of the Ancient World'.

Did the Babylonians go to war?

The Babylonian army was well trained and had good leaders. Both Hammurabi the Great and Nebuchadnezzar waged wars against surrounding lands. Skilled archers helped Nebuchadnezzar conquer lands, including Phoenicia, Syria, Judah and Assyria.

What were their houses like?

About 4,000 years ago, most people in Babylon had simple homes. However, rich people built large, flat-roofed houses with wooden balconies around a central courtyard. They lived in great comfort, with many servants to cook and clean for them.

Did they have gods?

The people of Babylon had many gods. Ishtar, the mother goddess, and Marduk, the dragon god, were the most powerful. One myth tells how the hero Gilgamesh's pride angered the gods, who sent a Bull of Heaven to destroy him – but Gilgamesh survived.

Who lost the secret of eternal life?

Legend tells how the Babylonian hero and king, Gilgamesh, was given the secret of eternal life – a plant from under the sea. He dived and picked the plant but he fell asleep on his way home. A snake gobbled up the plant and Gilgamesh lost the chance to live forever.

Quick-fire Quiz

1. Who was the mother goddess?
a) Marduk
b) Ishtar
c) Gilgamesh

2. How many laws did Hammurabi make?
a) 282
b) 272
c) 262

3. What ate the secret of life?
a) A snake
b) A bull
c) A genie

4. Who conquered Babylon in 539 BC?
a) The Greeks
b) The Egyptians
c) The Persians

What were genies?

The Babylonians believed that winged gods, or genies, protected royal palaces from demons and disease. This genie is holding a bucket and a pine cone, which were symbols of purification.

Who made good laws?

Hammurabi made 282 laws for his people to follow. Most were good laws, to protect the weak from the strong. They covered everything from fair rates of pay to rules for trading.

Did they keep pets?

Some Babylonians probably had domesticated cats and dogs, but rich people kept more exotic pets. The first zoos were owned by wealthy princes, who gave each other presents of wild animals such as lions and leopards.

Did Babylonians do maths?

Like earlier people in the region, the Babylonians used cuneiform writing, which can still be seen on clay tablets. Babylonian mathematicians worked out a system of counting based on the number 60. This was especially useful as 60 can be divided in many different ways. We still use this system today when we record the time (60 minutes in an hour, 60 seconds in a minute), and in measuring (there are 60 x 6 degrees in a circle). Babylonians recorded details of royal grants of land on boundary stones which deterred land disputes between neighbours. The Babylonians were also great astronomers.

Assyrians and Hittites

The Hittites from Anatolia (now in Turkey) conquered most of Syria, Mesopotamia and Babylon in the 1500s BC. Their empire fell in 1200 BC and the Assyrians, from northern Mesopotamia, took over. In 609 BC, the Assyrian empire fell to the Babylonians.

Who used battering rams?

Both the Hittites and the Assyrians were skilled at using siege warfare to defeat their enemies. Their armies would surround the enemy's city to stop food getting in. Then they used huge battering rams to knock holes in the city walls.

What did they build?

The Assyrians built magnificent cities, temples and palaces. The king often supervised the building from his chariot. Stones were brought from distant quarries, and oarsmen in skin boats towed laden rafts up the Tigris.

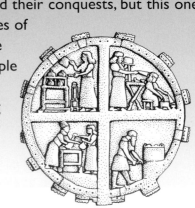

Who last ruled Assyria?

King Ashurbanipal was the last and greatest ruler of Assyria. He was a ruthless king, but he also built a great library where records and literature from Sumer and Babylon were stored on clay tablets. His palace at Nineveh had gardens stocked with plants from all over the world.

The Assyrian royal court

Who carved in stone?

The Hittites and Assyrians were great stone masons. The Hittites carved huge pictures of their gods and goddesses into the rock face near their temples. The Assyrians left many finely carved stone sculptures which tell us about their history and how they lived. Most of them show the kings and their conquests, but this one shows scenes of everyday life such as people preparing and cooking food.

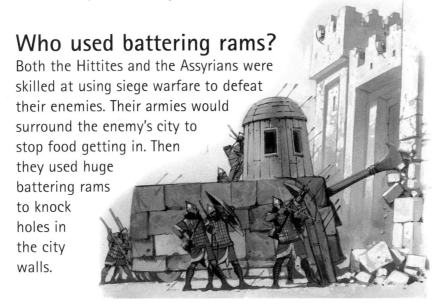

Carved stone being dragged to a new temple

Quick-fire Quiz

1. Who was Ashur?
a) A god
b) A king
c) A goddess

2. Where were the Hittites from?
a) Syria
b) Egypt
c) Anatolia

3. Where was Ashurbanipal's palace?
a) Babylon
b) Nineveh
c) Sumer

4. What animals pulled a war chariot?
a) Bulls
b) Lions
c) Horses

Winged lion

What gods did the Assyrians worship?

The Assyrians believed in many gods. Their chief god was Ashur whose name was used for their capital city. Ishtar was the Assyrians' goddess of war. The Babylonians also worshipped Ishtar, but believed that she was a mother-goddess who helped protect their city. To ward off evil spirits, huge stone sculptures of winged lions with human heads were placed on each side of important doors and gateways.

Who drove war chariots?

Both the Hittites and the Assyrians used war chariots in battle. The two-wheeled chariots were drawn by horses, and the skilled archers would fire at the enemy as they raced along. The Assyrians were fierce warriors, fighting with swords, slings, shields and bows.

Assyrian war chariot

Ancient Sea Traders

The Phoenicians were the best sea traders of the ancient world. They lived in city-states on the coast of the Mediterranean Sea (now Lebanon) from about 1200 to 146 BC. Their culture died out after the area was conquered by Alexander the Great.

Were the Phoenicians explorers?

The Phoenicians were skilled sailors and had fine ships. Around 600 BC, the Egyptians paid the Phoenicians to explore West Africa. They also sailed to Britain, where they traded goods for tin and silver.

What goods did Phoenicians trade?

Phoenician craftsmen made fine cloth as well as pottery, ivory and metal goods to sell. They also traded in the wood from cedar trees.

Who blew glass?

The Phoenicians were the first people to produce see-through glassware on a large scale. They also invented the process of glass blowing, which allowed them to make fine glassware like this.

Letters from the Phoenician alphabet

Could Phoenicians read and write?

The Phoenicians must have been able to read and write because they were among the first people to use an alphabet for writing words, rather than pictograms. Their alphabet was made up of 30 consonants — there were no vowels. These letters became the basis for all modern alphabets.

How did the Phoenicians get their name?

The name came from the Greek word 'phoinos' meaning 'red'. They were called this because they made a rich reddish-purple dye from a sea snail called a murex. Cloth dyed with this was expensive. In Roman times, only emperors were allowed to wear murex-dyed robes.

Murex

Quick-fire Quiz

1. What was made from a murex?
a) A dye
b) A food
c) A drink

2. Where was Carthage?
a) Spain
b) Africa
c) Greece

3. Who was the Phoenicians' main god?
a) Dido
b) Baal
c) Alexander

4. Where did Phoenicians explore?
a) America
b) Australia
c) Africa

Who founded the city of Carthage?

Carthage was the largest Phoenician city. According to legend, the founder of Carthage was the Phoenician princess Dido. After landing on the coast of North Africa, Dido asked the local ruler for land to build a city. He said she could take an area of land that could be enclosed by an ox-hide. Clever Dido had the hide cut into thin strips so that she could mark out a large plot of land. Carthage became one of the most important trading cities in the area.

Did they build temples?

The Phoenicians built many temples and shrines to their gods. Their main god was the warrior god Baal. There were priests and priestesses, who occasionally, in times of trouble, sacrificed children to the gods.

Phoenician priestess

Where were Phoenician colonies?

The Phoenicians spread throughout the Mediterranean, setting up colonies in many foreign lands including Marseilles (France), Cadiz (Spain), Malta, Sicily, Cyprus and Carthage (now Tunisia) in North Africa. From Carthage they traded with local Africans, buying precious ivory, animal skins and wood.

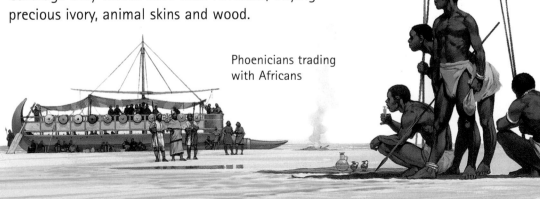

Phoenicians trading with Africans

Ancient Greece

By 500 BC, ancient Greece was made up of small, independent city-states around the Mediterranean. Each city-state had its own government and laws. The most important of these city-states were Athens and Sparta.

Who were the Spartans?

The city-state of Sparta in southern Greece was a mighty military power. All Spartan men were in the army, and boys left home at seven to start training as soldiers. Women did not fight, but they had to be very fit so their babies would be healthy and strong.

What was an acropolis?

Each Greek city-state had a walled city with an acropolis (fort) and an agora — a large open space used for meetings and markets. In time the acropolis became a religious centre.

Who left Athens?

Criminals or unpopular politicians could be banished (ostracized). Each year, Athenians could write the name of a person they wanted banished on bits of pottery called 'ostraka'. Anyone with more than 6,000 votes had to leave for 10 years!

Did Greeks play sports?

The ancient Greeks enjoyed competitive games. The Olympics – the most famous – were first held in 776 BC, and took place every four years. At first, there was just one race. By 500 BC, the Games lasted five days.

Who won an olive wreath?

On the final day of the Olympic Games the winners received their prizes – crowns of laurel leaves or wild olives cut from a special grove near the temple of Zeus. Afterwards they were guests of honour at a victory feast.

Who played outdoors?

Greek plays were performed in large open-air theatres. The semicircular theatre in Athens held over 10,000 people. All the actors were male, and they wore brightly painted masks to show which characters they were playing.

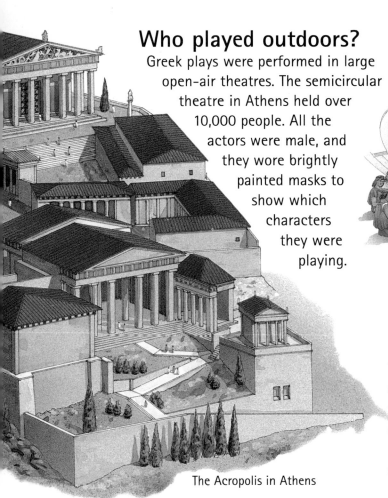

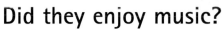
The Acropolis in Athens

Did they enjoy music?

The Greeks enjoyed singing and dancing, and music was played on most social occasions. Poetry was chanted, accompanied by music, or sung. The main stringed instrument was the lyre, which was sometimes made from a tortoise shell.

Who read the future?

The Greeks had many gods. The chief was Zeus who lived on Mount Olympus, the highest mountain in Greece. If the Greeks wanted to ask the gods about the future, they visited oracles. Priests and priestesses at an oracle spoke on behalf of the gods. The advice from the gods was usually so vague that it always seemed to be right. The most famous oracle was in the temple of the sun god, Apollo, at Delphi.

Whose speeches were timed?

In Athens, all men who were not slaves were citizens, and could speak at the Assembly. At this meeting they could give their opinions on political matters. Each speaker was timed with a water clock, so he could not talk for too long!

Quick-fire Quiz

1. What foretold the future?
a) The Assembly
b) An acropolis
c) An oracle

2. What was a lyre?
a) A bird
b) A musical instrument
c) An Olympic sport

3. How often were the Olympic Games held?
a) Every year
b) Every four years
c) Every ten years

4. Who could speak at the Assembly?
a) Citizens
b) Slaves
c) Everyone

Greek Life

Greek architecture, the arts, sport and science flourished during the Golden Age (600 to 300 BC). Athens became the centre of Greek culture. In 338 BC, King Philip of Macedonia conquered Greece. His son, Alexander the Great, spread Greek learning to North Africa and the Middle East.

Where did people shop?

In the agora, or marketplace, you could buy everything from food to fabrics, silverware to slaves. Fast-food sellers supplied tasty snacks, and you could even visit a doctor.

What were Greek houses like?

Greek houses were made of sun-dried, mud bricks built round a central courtyard. Most houses were single storey, but some wealthier homes had bedrooms on a second floor. Greek men, women and slaves all lived in separate quarters.

How do we know about ancient Greek life?

Archaeologists have found marble and bronze statues and pottery bowls, vases and cups decorated with scenes from Greek life. These tell us what the Greeks wore and how they lived.

What did ancient Greeks eat?

Basic foods were bread, olives, figs and goats' milk cheese. Meat was expensive but fish was cheap along the coast. Women prepared the food, and everyone ate in the courtyard.

What did Greeks wear?

Everyone wore a chiton – a large cloth rectangle fastened at the shoulders. Saffron yellow was a favourite colour, but purple, red and violet were also fashionable. Wealthy women piled their hair into elaborate styles, and wore make-up, earrings, necklaces, bracelets and rings.

Did Greeks have baths?

Few homes had baths, but the gymnasium, a public sports ground in Athens, had plunge pools and steam baths. Women and children washed using bronze basins, and some homes had terracotta hip baths. Slaves helped their masters to wash.

Where did people relax?

The agora was a place to relax and meet friends. Men met there to listen to storytellers recounting tales, or to hear philosophers such as Socrates discuss politics.

Quick-fire Quiz

1. What was an agora?
a) A school
b) A marketplace
c) A temple

2. Who went to school?
a) Boys
b) Girls
c) No-one

3. What was a chiton?
a) A stool
b) A book
c) A robe

4. Who conquered Greece in 338 BC?
a) Philip
b) Alexander
c) Socrates

Did they have furniture?

Wealthy Athenians lived in heated homes with fine furniture. They lounged on padded couches and ate from small tables inlaid with ivory. Their wooden beds had leather thongs to support a mattress, and lots of cushions.

Did Greek children go to school?

Rich Athenian boys went to school between the ages of seven and 18. They studied maths, reading, writing, music and poetry in the morning and did athletics and dancing in the afternoon. The girls stayed at home, learning to spin, weave and run a household.

The Persians

About 3,000 years ago, Persia (Iran) was ruled by two powers, the Medes and the Persians. In 550 BC, Persian king, Cyrus the Great, seized power. He made Persia the centre of a huge empire, which lasted until 330 BC, when Alexander the Great took control.

Who was Alexander the Great?
Alexander the Great became king of Greece in 336 BC, and set out to conquer the Persians. He was a great soldier and a clever leader. Within 12 years he had taken over Persia, and built an empire stretching from Egypt to India.

Who made Persia great?
King Darius I ruled Persia from 521 to 486 BC. His powerful empire included Egypt and the Indus Valley. He taxed all the people he conquered, and the tributes they brought him included food, animals, fine cloth, gold and jewels. He built roads to link the empire, and introduced a standard currency to increase trade.

What sort of religion did the Persians have?

Many Persians worshipped Mithras, the god of light, truth and justice. There was a legend that he killed a magic bull, and that every animal and plant sprang from its blood. Later, Mithras was popular with Roman soldiers, who built temples to him. A Persian prophet called Zoroaster, who lived around 600 BC, founded a new religion, Zoroastrianism, which is still followed today in parts of Iran and India.

Quick-fire Quiz

1. Who founded the Persian empire?
a) King Cyrus
b) King Darius
c) King Philip

2. When was the Battle of Salamis?
a) 380 BC
b) 480 BC
c) 580 BC

3. Who or what was Zoroaster?
a) A palace
b) A city
c) A prophet

4. What was a trireme?
a) A god
b) A sword
c) A ship

Who were the Parthians?

The Parthians moved into Persia in about 1000 BC and lived under Persian rule. After the death of Alexander the Great, the Parthians took over the area. A favourite trick of Parthian archers was to pretend to retreat, then turn in their saddles to fire back at the enemy – the origin of the saying 'a Parthian shot'.

Did Persia have an army?

The Persians had a large, well-trained army. The soldiers were armed with spears, daggers and bows and arrows. They wore leather tunics strengthened with scales to protect them in battle.

Did the Persians and Greeks fight?

The Greeks and Persians were at war for many years. At the Battle of Salamis, in 480 BC, the Persian fleet was forced to retreat by the might of the Greek triremes. A trireme was a swift ship powered by more than 150 oarsmen grouped in threes on either side of the ship.

Was Persia rich?

Persia became very rich under Darius I, who lived in a huge palace in Persepolis. The Great Hall alone held 10,000 people. When Alexander the Great invaded, he is said to have taken 4,500 tonnes of gold from the Persian cities of Persepolis and Susa.

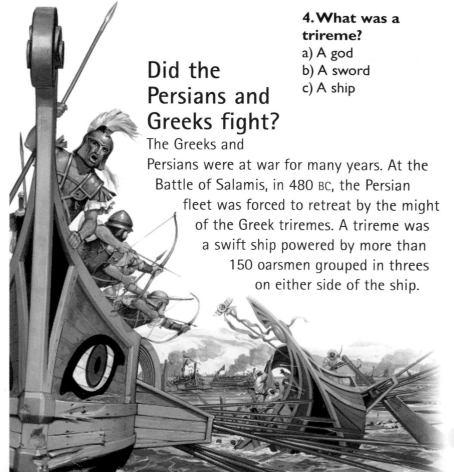

Ancient China

The first emperor of China was King Zheng of Qin. In 221 BC, he defeated the rulers of all the states that made up China, and founded the Qin dynasty, from which China gets its name. The Han dynasty (206 BC to AD 220) opened up trade with the West.

What is a dynasty?

China was governed by a series of ruling families, called dynasties. The Zhou dynasty ruled China for over 800 years from 1122 BC. Zhou society was divided into nobles, peasants and slaves. Iron was first used at this time, and farming methods improved.

Who was Confucius?

Confucius, or K'ung Fu-tzu, was born in China in 551 BC. He was a great thinker who believed that the emperor should care for his people like a father, and that the people should love and obey him. For over 2,000 years his teachings influenced the way China was ruled.

What was the terracotta army?

When King Zheng became emperor, he changed his name to Shi Huangdi ('first emperor') and ordered a splendid tomb to be built. His tomb was guarded by a terracotta army – 7,000 life-size clay soldiers. The soldiers had real crossbows and spears, with life-size clay horses and chariots.

Who invented paper?

Chinese inventors discovered many useful things. Around AD 100, a man called Tsai Lung rolled a paste of hemp and wood into a sheet which he stretched and dried. He had invented paper! About 800 years later, the Chinese printed the first banknotes.

What are Yin and Yang?

The Chinese believe everything in nature is in harmony. Confucius depicted this by the Yin and Yang symbol. The dark Yin interlocks with the light Yang, and each one contains a tiny bit of the other.

Who invented the compass?

The ancient Chinese were great scientists and inventors. During the Han dynasty, scientists invented the first magnetic compass with a dial and a pointer. At first, they did not use it for navigation, as we do now, but to make sure that their temples faced the right way. The Chinese were very skilled sailors. Hundreds of years before the Europeans, the Chinese built sea-going ships with lots of sails and steered by rudders. Chinese sailors travelled as far as Africa to trade. They were also skilled mathematicians and astronomers. The Chinese were the first to make maps using a grid system, and to work out that a year has 365.25 days.

Who built the Great Wall?

The Great Wall of China was built for Shi Huangdi between 214 and 204 BC, by thousands of poor farmers. Short bits of wall were joined up to make the longest wall in the world, stretching over 2,200 kilometres. The wall is up to 15 metres high, and is wide enough for a bus to drive along the top.

Who defeated an emperor?

Life was hard for most peasants during the Qin dynasty. They had to pay taxes and work for Shi Huangdi. After his death, the peasants rebelled against the new emperor, his son. They raised a large army and, in 209 BC, the emperor was defeated.

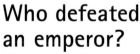

Peasants during the Qin Dynasty

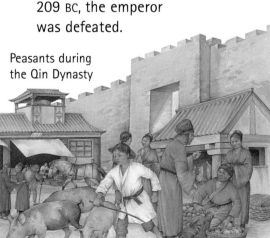

Quick-fire Quiz

1. What did the terracotta army guard?
a) A palace
b) A tomb
c) A city

2. Who invented paper?
a) K'ung Fu-tzu
b) Shi Huangdi
c) Tsai Lung

3. How high is the Great Wall?
a) 25m
b) 15m
c) 5m

4. When was Confucius born?
a) 551 BC
b) 151 BC
c) 51 BC

The Celts

Between 750 and 50 BC, the Celts were the most important tribes in Europe. There were many different Celtic tribes, but they all spoke the same kind of language and had similar lifestyles. Eventually, the Romans conquered most of their lands.

What were Celtic homes like?

A Celtic house often had walls made of branches covered with clay, and a thatched roof of straw or reeds. Most homes had one large room, where the family cooked, ate and slept. There were no windows. A central fire provided heat and light.

Were the Celts warriors?

Celtic men and women were renowned fighters and battles between tribes were common! Many warriors painted their faces and bodies blue to look as fierce as possible. Some went into battle naked but others wore tartan tops, capes and trousers, and carried fine bronze shields.

Were the Celts interested in arts and crafts?

The Celts were great poets and musicians and made beautifully decorated metalwork. Wealthy warriors carried fine shields, and often wore an armband made from gold and a delicately carved neck ring, called a torque. Celtic jewellery and weapons were decorated with abstract or geometrical designs.

Shield

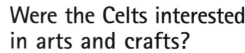

Armband

Were cattle important?

The Celts were farmers. They depended on meat to get them through the winter, so cattle were very important. At the feast of Beltane on May 1, which marked the start of summer, Druids (priests) chased cattle through bonfires to expel evil spirits and disease.

A bull's head decoration from a cauldron found in Denmark

What are Celtic myths about?

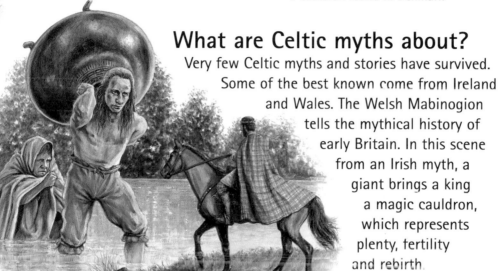

Very few Celtic myths and stories have survived. Some of the best known come from Ireland and Wales. The Welsh Mabinogion tells the mythical history of early Britain. In this scene from an Irish myth, a giant brings a king a magic cauldron, which represents plenty, fertility and rebirth.

Quick-fire Quiz

1. What was a torque?
a) An earring
b) A neck ring
c) A belt

2. When was Beltane celebrated?
a) November
b) February
c) May

3. What was a Druid?
a) A priest
b) A warrior
c) A king

4. What is Stonehenge?
a) A feast
b) A city
c) A monument

Who built Stonehenge?

Stonehenge in England was built by Stone Age people in around 2750 BC, long before the Celts. The layout of the huge circle of standing stones marked the midsummer sunrise and the midwinter moonrise. Historians think this monument was used as a place of worship and to study the stars. Later, Celts may have used it as a meeting place for worship and to make sacrifices to their gods.

Could Celts read and write?

Celts did not read or write. Their myths, laws and religion were passed down by word of mouth. Druids taught poetry, history and the law. At feasts, musicians and storytellers called bards told tales of brave heroes.

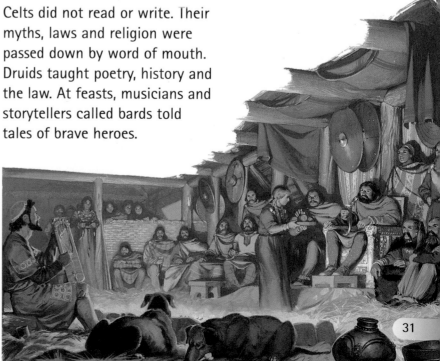

Life in Ancient Rome

At first, ancient Rome was ruled by kings, but in 509 BC the Romans set up a republic with elected leaders. Rome gradually took over other lands, and by AD 150 the empire stretched across Europe into Africa.

Who were looked after by wolves?

According to Roman legend, a king named Numitor had two baby grandsons, called Romulus and Remus. They were thrown into the River Tiber, but a wolf rescued them and brought them up. When they grew up, the brothers built Rome.

Where did rich Romans live?

Many rich Romans had a country home (a villa) and a town house (a domus). Houses were built around a courtyard and had lots of rooms, running water, a kitchen, central heating and sometimes even a bathroom.

Did Romans wear make-up?

A rich Roman lady powdered her face with chalk or white lead and painted her lips with red ochre. She took a long time to get ready for the day, even though slave girls helped her dress and style her hair.

Who ruled Rome?

The Roman republic was ruled by the Senate – a group of elder citizens. Each year, the Senate elected two consuls to lead Rome. The Senate met to decide how Rome was to be run and to advise the consuls, who were the most powerful people in Rome.

Where did the poor live?

Romans with little money lived in tiny flats in high-rise buildings. Many buildings were not very stable, and sometimes fell down with the people still inside. The flats had no kitchens or gardens, so people had to buy hot food from take-aways, and string washing between the buildings. They threw their rubbish into the streets, making the city dirty and smelly. Water had to be collected from a public water trough. Only rich people had piped water in their homes.

Gladiator

Did rich Romans have feasts?

Rich Romans really enjoyed having friends round for a feast. They served dozens of tasty dishes such as oysters, stuffed dormice, roast peacock and boiled ostrich. The Romans did not sit on chairs to eat, instead they lounged on couches. They ate with their fingers or with a spoon. Some rich Romans were so greedy they tried every dish and, in order to make room for more, they made themselves sick. They even had a special room for people to be sick in. It was called the vomitorium!

Who fought for sport?

The Romans loved to go to the amphitheatre to watch violent shows, which they called 'games'. At the amphitheatre, gladiators fought each other, often to the death. Some gladiators had to fight wild animals, such as lions, with spears, flaming torches or even their bare hands.

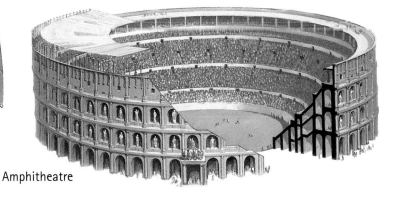
Amphitheatre

Quick-fire Quiz

1. When did Rome become a republic?
a) 509 BC
b) 409 BC
c) 309 BC

2. Who ruled the republic?
a) The emperor
b) The Senate
c) The king

3. What was a gladiator?
a) A public bath
b) A country house
c) A fighter

4. Who brought up Romulus and Remus?
a) Rich ladies
b) A wolf
c) The consuls

Where did Romans relax?

Most Romans went to the public baths to relax. These were more like leisure centres than places to wash. You could play games, read, chat to friends, work out in the gym or take a stroll in the gardens. You could even get your hair cut or have a massage.

33

The Roman Empire

The Roman republic ended in 27 BC, when Emperor Augustus set up a Roman empire. However, in AD 395 the empire was split into two. The western part (based in Rome) fell to tribes the Romans called 'barbarians' in AD 476. The eastern part, ruled from Constantinople (now Istanbul) lasted until AD 1453.

Did the Romans build bridges?

The Romans were very clever builders and engineers. They built huge stone bridges called viaducts to carry roads, and aqueducts (stone channels to carry water) across valleys. They also built many fine cities, linking them with long, straight roads.

Which Roman leader was murdered?

Julius Caesar was a great general who made himself dictator (sole ruler) for life. Although he brought peace and passed good laws, the Senate thought he was too powerful. So on March 15, 44 BC, a group of them stabbed him to death.

Julius Caesar

What did the Romans trade?

Roman trade routes spread throughout Europe and into China and India. Their ships took many goods such as wine, olive oil and farm products as well as works of art to distant ports. They brought back exotic goods such as wild animals, ivory and silk.

Roman ship

Where did Roman soldiers live?

Soldiers on the move lived in leather tents. At other times, they lived in large forts with workshops, stables and hospitals. The men shared simple rooms, but the officers had houses.

How did Romans protect their cities?

In later times, the Romans needed to protect their cities from attack by the barbarian tribes that swept across Europe. They built thick walls around their towns and forts which could be defended easily by armed soldiers.

What did Roman soldiers wear?

Roman soldiers wore armour of metal strips joined together with straps, over a woollen tunic. They carried a shield to protect the lower body. On the move, they carried everything on their backs – weapons, tools and a kit bag.

Why was Rome so successful?

A well-organized, full-time army was the key to Rome's success. Highly trained soldiers were split into legions of 6,000 men made up of ten cohorts, and then into centuries of 100 men, under the command of a centurion (officer).

Who met in the catacombs?

Early Christians were persecuted by the Romans who thought they were plotting against the emperor. The Christians met in secret in the catacombs (underground burial chambers) beneath Rome. Many Christians were put to death in the arena to entertain the crowds. Some were made to fight unarmed against gladiators or lions. Emperor Constantine was converted to Christianity in AD 313, and about 60 years later it became the empire's official religion.

How were soldiers like a tortoise?

When they attacked an enemy fort, Roman soldiers protected themselves by forming a 'testudo' (tortoise). They held their shields over their heads so that they overlapped.

Who attacked Rome with elephants?

In 218 BC, Hannibal, a military leader from Carthage in North Africa, led 10,000 soldiers and 38 elephants through Spain and across the Alps to attack Rome. Hannibal won three important victories but only 12 elephants survived.

Quick-fire Quiz

1. Who attacked Rome on elephants?
a) Augustus
b) Hannibal
c) Caesar

2. What was a centurion?
a) An officer
b) A politician
c) A senator

3. What does an aqueduct carry?
a) Oil
b) Wine
c) Water

4. What are catacombs?
a) High-rise flats
b) Public baths
c) Burial chambers

The Mayan Empire

The Maya Indians built a vast empire that covered parts of Mexico, Guatemala and Honduras in the jungles of Central America. It reached its peak from AD 300–800 but, over the next 200 years, it collapsed and was taken over by the Toltecs.

What clothes did Mayans wear?

Mayan men wore simple loin cloths. If it was cold they also wore a cloak called a 'manta'. Men dressed up in elaborate headdresses decorated with quetzal or macaw feathers. The more important the person, the bigger his hat! Women wore simple smock-like dresses.

God-king　　Noble　　Warrior　　Priest

Who ruled the Maya?

Every Mayan city-state had its own royal family. They were ruled by a warrior god-king who led his people into battle. Next in importance were nobles, warriors and priests. Then came craftsmen and merchants, and last were peasants and labourers. The Maya worshipped the jaguar and noble Mayan warriors wore jaguar skins and headdresses. They thought that this would help to make them as fierce and brave in battle as a jaguar.

What were Mayan cities like?

The Maya were the first people in America to build big cities. These cities, which lay deep in the jungle, were full of grand pyramids, temples and palaces built of local limestone. The walls were covered with plaster and sometimes painted red. This colour was especially important to the Maya, for religious reasons. Walls were sometimes decorated with paintings of gods and hieroglyphs.

Did the Maya build pyramids?

The Maya built huge, stone-stepped pyramids with temples and an observatory at the top. The Castillo, the main pyramid in the Mayan city of Chichen Itza, has four stairways, each with 91 steps. These, together with the step at the temple entrance, add up to 365 – the number of days in a year.

Did Mayans study the stars?

The Maya were expert astronomers and studied the moon, stars and planets. They were also skilled mathematicians, and had a complicated calendar for counting the days and years. They used their knowledge to predict special events such as an eclipse.

Could Mayans read and write?

The Maya wrote in hieroglyphs (picture writing). They carved important inscriptions on huge stone monuments called stelae. They also wrote detailed accounts of important events in books made of bark or on animal skins. When the Spanish conquered the area in the early 1500s, they burned most of these books.

Quick-fire Quiz

1. What is the Castillo?
a) A city
b) A pyramid
c) A book

2. What was a 'manta'?
a) A hat
b) A dress
c) A cloak

3. What were Mayan cities built from?
a) Limestone
b) Mud
c) Wood

4. What were stelae?
a) Monuments
b) Temples
c) Priests

Did the Maya play ball?

The Maya played a religious ball game called Pok-a-tok. The players, who were bandaged to prevent injury, bounced a solid rubber ball to each other using their elbows, hips and thighs. The game was won by the first team to hit the ball through a stone ring mounted on the wall.

What gods did they worship?

The Mayans had over 150 gods. The most important was the sun god, who went down into the Underworld at sunset and became the jaguar god. They sometimes sacrificed captured enemies to their gods.

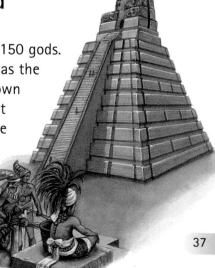

Timeline

Key dates in the development of ancient civilizations are recorded here – from the first cave paintings, through the creation and establishment of great empires to the sacking of Rome by the Vandals.

25,000 BC to 2000 BC

c.25,000 BC Stone Age people painted cave walls

c.10,000–9000 BC Start of agriculture in Near East

8000–7000 BC First permanent houses built; walled cities developed in Near East and Turkey

6000–5000 BC Looms used for weaving in Near East

5000 BC People began farming in Nile Valley in Egypt

4000–3000 BC Sumerian civilization in Mesopotamia; invented cuneiform writing; used ploughs and wheel

3372 BC First date in Mayan calendar

3000 BC Lower and Upper Egypt united under a single pharaoh

3000 BC Troy flourished as a city-state in Anatolia

c.2800 BC Stonehenge built in England

2800–2400 BC City-states of Sumer at their most powerful

2500 BC Rise of Indus Valley people

2700–2200 BC Old Kingdom in Egypt; first step pyramids built

2690 BC Huang Ti (Yellow emperor) ruled in China; according to legend, silk was discovered by his wife Hsi-Ling Shi

2600 BC Sphinx and Great Pyramids built in Egypt

2500 BC First European civilization, the Minoans, grew up on Greek island of Crete

2360 BC Arabians migrated to Mesopotamia and set up Babylonian and Assyrian kingdoms

2250 BC Hsai dynasty in power in China

2050 BC Start of Middle Kingdom of Egypt

2000 BC Hittites arrived in Anatolia (now Turkey)

2000 BC Mycenaeans invaded Greece

1999 BC to 1000 BC

1925 BC Hittites conquered Babylon

1830 BC First dynasty of Babylonian empire founded

1814–1782 BC Assyria extended empire

1792–1750 BC Hammurabi the Great ruled Babylon; empire declined after his death

1760 BC Shang dynasty founded in China

1750–1500 BC Hittites spread throughout area; invaded Syria

1650–1450 BC Mycenaean power centred on Mycenae and Pylos

1550–1050 BC New Kingdom in Egypt; Valley of Kings used for pharaohs' tombs

1500–1166 BC Egypt at peak of power

1500 BC Aryans invaded Indus Valley

c1500 BC Mayans farm land in Central America; developed a calendar and writing

1450 BC Minoan civilization collapsed and Mycenaeans took over

1350–1250 BC Assyrian empire extends

1200 BC Trojan Wars: Mycenaeans invaded and destroyed Troy in Anatolia

1200 BC Hittites' empire collapsed after invasion of Phoenicians; Phoenicians became the world's most powerful sea traders

1150 BC Israelites arrived in Canaan

1100 BC Mycenaean civilization collapsed

c.1122 BC Zhou dynasty in China came to power after defeating armies of Shang dynasty

1050 BC Phoenicians developed alphabet (basis for all modern alphabets)

c.1000 BC Dorians invaded Greece; start of Dark Ages

c.1000 BC Kingdom of Kush in Africa began

1000 BC Israel ruled by King David

999 BC to 500 BC

900–625 BC Assyria and Babylon at war

900–700 BC Etruscans flourished in upper Italy

c.814 BC Carthage founded

800 BC Greek poet Homer wrote about Trojan Wars and Greek legends

800 BC Olmecs in Mexico built temples

753 BC Traditional date for founding of Rome

750–600 BC Celts appeared in Central Europe and spread throughout western Europe

c.750–682 BC Kingdom of Kush defeated Egypt; Nubians rule over Egypt

729 BC Assyrians ruled Babylon

700 BC Assyrians took over Phoenicia and Israel

700–500 BC Rise of Athens and other Greek city-states

689 BC Assyrians destroyed Babylon

671–664 BC Assyrians ruled Egypt

668–627 BC Assurbanipal increased power of Assyria

609 BC Assyrian empire ended

605–562 BC Nebuchadnezzar rebuilt Babylon

c.600 BC Zoroaster reforms the ancient Persian religion

590 BC Babylonians took over Jerusalem

c.550 BC Persian empire became powerful

551 BC Confucius was born in China

539 BC Persians took over Babylon and Phoenicia

525–404 BC Persians ruled Egypt

509 BC Roman kings replaced by Roman republic

508 BC Athens became a democracy

500 BC Italian Etruscan empire very powerful

499 BC to AD 1

490–480 BC Persian wars between Greeks and Persians; Greeks defeated Persians in 479 BC

c.477–405 BC Golden Age of Athens

463–221 BC Time of warring states in China

450–400 BC Etruscan empire declined

431–404 BC Peloponnesian wars between Athens and Sparta; Sparta won in 404 BC

390 BC Celts attacked Rome

338 BC Philip of Macedonia conquered Greece

336 BC Alexander the Great became king of Macedonia and Greece

333–323 BC Alexander the Great conquered Phoenicia, Egypt, Persia and parts of India

321–184 BC Mauryan empire founded in India

300 BC Mayans started to build stone cities

275 BC Romans took over all Italy

265 BC Romans started to conquer Europe

264–146 BC Carthage at war with Rome (Punic Wars)

250 BC Celtic tribes at peak of power

221 BC Emperor Qin united China in first dynasty

206 BC– AD 220 Han dynasty in China

218 BC Hannibal invaded Rome on elephants

202 BC Hannibal defeated by Romans

146 BC Carthage defeated; North Africa became part of Roman empire

55 BC Julius Caesar invaded Britain but had to retreat

52 BC Caesar conquered Celtic Gaul (France)

45 BC Caesar became dictator of Rome

44 BC Caesar assassinated

30 BC Egypt taken over by the Romans

27 BC Octavian becomes first Roman emperor, Augustus

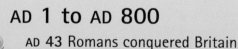

AD 1 to AD 800

AD 43 Romans conquered Britain

AD 61 Celtic Queen Boudicca led revolt against Romans in Britain

AD 64 Rome destroyed by fire

AD 79 Mount Vesuvius erupted covering Pompeii (Roman city) in ash

c.AD 150 Roman empire most powerful

AD 250 European barbarian tribes attacked Rome

AD 284 Roman empire split into east and west

AD 268 Goths sacked Athens and Sparta

AD 330 Constantinople (now Istanbul) became capital of eastern Roman empire

AD 300–700 Mayan civilization at height

AD 406 Tribe called Vandals overran Gaul

AD 410 Rome sacked by Visigoths; Romans left Britain

AD 455 Rome sacked by Vandals

AD 476 Last western Roman emperor deposed; eastern empire continued until AD 1453 as Byzantine empire

AD 800 Mayan cities abandoned; civilization collapsed; Toltecs took over

Index

acropolis 22
Africa 4, 20, 21, 24, 32, 35
Alexander the Great 20, 24, 26, 27
aqueduct 34
arts 4, 8, 15, 18, 20, 23, 30
Ashurbanipal, King 18
Assyrians 18–19
Augustus, Emperor 34

Babylon 16–17, 18, 19
barbarians 34, 35
baths 25, 33
Britain 20, 31

Caesar, Julius 34
Celts 30–31
chariots 6, 18, 19
Chinese 28–29
cities 4, 6, 21, 22, 34, 35, 36
    Athens 22
    Babylon 16
    Carthage 21, 35
    Çatal Hüyük 4
    Chichen Itza 37
    Constantinople 34
    Harappa 6
    Knossus 14
    Mohenjo-daro 6
    Nineveh 18
    Persepolis 27
    Pylos 15
    Sparta 22
    Ur 7
clothes 4, 7, 8, 21, 24, 30, 32, 36

Confucius (K'ung Fu-Tzu) 28
Crete (Greece) 14, 15
Cyrus, King 26

Darius, King 26, 27
Delphi 23
Druids 31

Egyptians 8–13, 20
emperors 28, 34
Europe 14, 30, 35

farming 4, 5, 6, 9, 31
food 4, 5, 6, 8, 24, 26, 33

games 7, 15, 22, 33, 37
genies 17
Gilgamesh, King 17
gladiators 33
gods 4, 9, 10, 11, 17, 18, 19, 21,
    23, 27, 31, 36, 37
    Anubis 11
    Apollo 23
    Ashur 19
    Baal 21
    Bastet 10
    Beltane 31
    Ishtar 17, 19
    Marduk 17
    Mithras 27
    Sun 37
    Zeus 23
Great Wall of China 29
Greeks 21, 22–25, 27

Hammurabi, King 16, 17

Han dynasty 28, 29
Hannibal 35
hieroglyphs 8, 11, 37
Hittites 18–19
houses 4, 5, 6, 7, 24, 30, 32, 33
hunting 4, 14

Indus (Pakistan) 6, 7
inventions 17, 28, 29

Mayans 36–37
Mediterranean 20, 21
Mesopotamia 6, 7, 16, 18
Minoans 14–15
Minos, King 14
minotaur 14
mummies 10–11
    embalming 10, 11
music 7, 8, 23
Mycenaeans 14, 15

Nebuchadnezzar, King 16
Nestor, King 15
Numitar, King 32
Nile, River 6, 8, 9

Olympic Games 22
oracle 23

palaces 14, 15, 18, 36
Parthians 27
Persians 26–27
pharaohs 9, 11, 12–13
    Khufu 13
    Menes 9
    Tutankhamun 11, 13

Philip, King 24
Phoenicians 20–21
priests 10, 21, 31, 37
pyramids 12–13, 36, 37

Qin dynasty 28, 29

Remus 32
Romans 21, 30, 32–35
Romulus 32

school 25
scribes 8
Senate 32, 34
soldiers 15, 16, 18, 22, 27, 28,
    30, 34, 35
Spartans 22
sports 22, 25, 33, 37
Stonehenge 31
Sumer 6–7, 18
Syria 18

temples 7, 12, 13, 18, 21, 36, 37
theatre 23
Toltecs 36
tombs 10, 11, 12–13, 28
toys 8
trade 7, 9, 14, 20, 21, 26, 34

wheel 6
writing 6, 8, 20, 31, 37
    cuneiform 6
    hieroglyphs 8, 11, 37

Zheng, King 28
ziggurats 7
Zoroaster 27

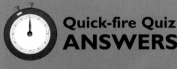

Quick-fire Quiz
ANSWERS

Page 5 The First Peoples
1.c 2.a 3.b 4.a

Page 7 River Valley Civilizations
1.b 2.a 3.c 4.c

Page 9 Ancient Egypt
1.b 2.b 3.c 4.b

Page 11 Priests and Mummies
1.b 2.a 3.b 4.c

Page 13 Pyramids and Tombs
1.b 2.a 3.c 4.b

Page 15 Crete and Mycenae
1.c 2.b 3.c 4.a

Page 17 Babylon
1.b 2.a 3.a 4.c

Page 19 Assyrians and Hittites
1.a 2.c 3.b 4.c

Page 21 Ancient Sea Traders
1.a 2.b 3.b 4.c

Page 23 Ancient Greece
1.c 2.b 3.b 4.a

Page 25 Greek Life
1.b 2.a 3.c 4.a

Page 27 The Persians
1.a 2.b 3.c 4.c

Page 29 Ancient China
1.b 2.c 3.b 4.a

Page 31 The Celts
1.b 2.c 3.a 4.c

Page 33 Life in Ancient Rome
1.a 2.b 3.c 4.b

Page 35 The Roman Empire
1.b 2.a 3.c 4.c

Page 37 The Mayan Empire
1.b 2.c 3.a 4.a